My Spelling Workbook

Prim-Ed
Publishing

My Spelling Workbook – Book C
© R.I.C. Publications

Australia: PO Box 332, Greenwood, Western Australia 6924
Republic of Ireland: Marshmeadows, New Ross, Co. Wexford, Ireland

First Published in 1990, R.I.C. Publications
Revised and Reprinted 2001, 2010, 2014 Prim-Ed Publishing

ISBN 978-1-86400-402-1

Introduction

Welcome to My Spelling Workbook. This book has lots of different activities to help you improve your spelling. Here are some tips to show you the best way to use your book.

- **Learning Words**

    Each list of words in the book has five test columns. Every time you spell a word correctly in a test, you can tick the column.

    Three ticks in a row shows that you know how to spell the word.

    If you do not get three ticks in a row, you write 'T' in the transfer box. When you start your next list of words, you add the word to the table 'Difficult Words I Have Found'. You can also add any other difficult words you find.

- **Look, Say, Trace, Cover, Write, Check**

    These words are to remind you of the best way to learn to spell.
    You should follow this when you are learning each word.

- **Recording your Scores**

    At the back of the book, you will find a grid for recording your scores for each unit. This will help you to keep track of how you are improving with your spelling.

- **How to Become a Better Speller**

    1. *Have a go!*
       Write the word on the piece of paper.
       Does it look right? If it doesn't look right, try writing it another way.

    2. *Look around your classroom*
       There are probably many words around you that you just didn't notice.

    3. *Use a dictionary, personal dictionary or spelling calculator*
       Try using these before you ask a teacher.

    4. *Ask the teacher, another adult or a friend*
       If you have tried the first three, then ask someone else for help.

Contents

Unit 1 2–5	Unit 13 50–53
Unit 2 6–9	Unit 14 54–57
Unit 3 10–13	Unit 15 58–61
Unit 4 14–17	Unit 16 62–65
Unit 5 18–21	Unit 17 66–69
Unit 6 22–25	Unit 18 70–73
Unit 7 26–29	Interesting Words from my Writing 74–75
Unit 8 30–33	My Dictionary Words: Aa to Ii 76
Unit 9 34–37	My Dictionary Words: Jj to Rr 77
Unit 10 38–41	My Dictionary Words: Ss to Zz 78
Unit 11 42–45	Recording Grid
Unit 12 46–49	

UNIT 1

List Words	Test 1	Test 2	Test 3	Test 4	Test 5	T
cable						
data						
input						
job						
output						
disc						
save						
spray						
belt						
felt						
seal						
real						
fear						
bay						
euro						
today						
yesterday						
away						

Look Say Trace Cover Write Check

Difficult Words I Have Found	Test 1	Test 2	Test 3	T

What am I?

1. I am made from leather.

   I have many holes.

   I go around your waist.

   I am a _____

Rhyming Words

2. Choose a rhyming word from your list.

   (a) meal _____

   (b) gave _____

   (c) tear _____

   (d) fable _____

   (e) rob _____

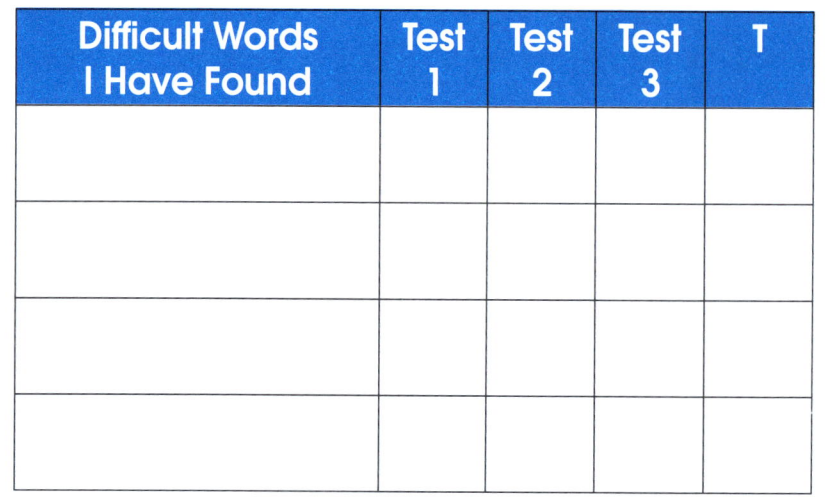

3. Use list words to solve the crossword.

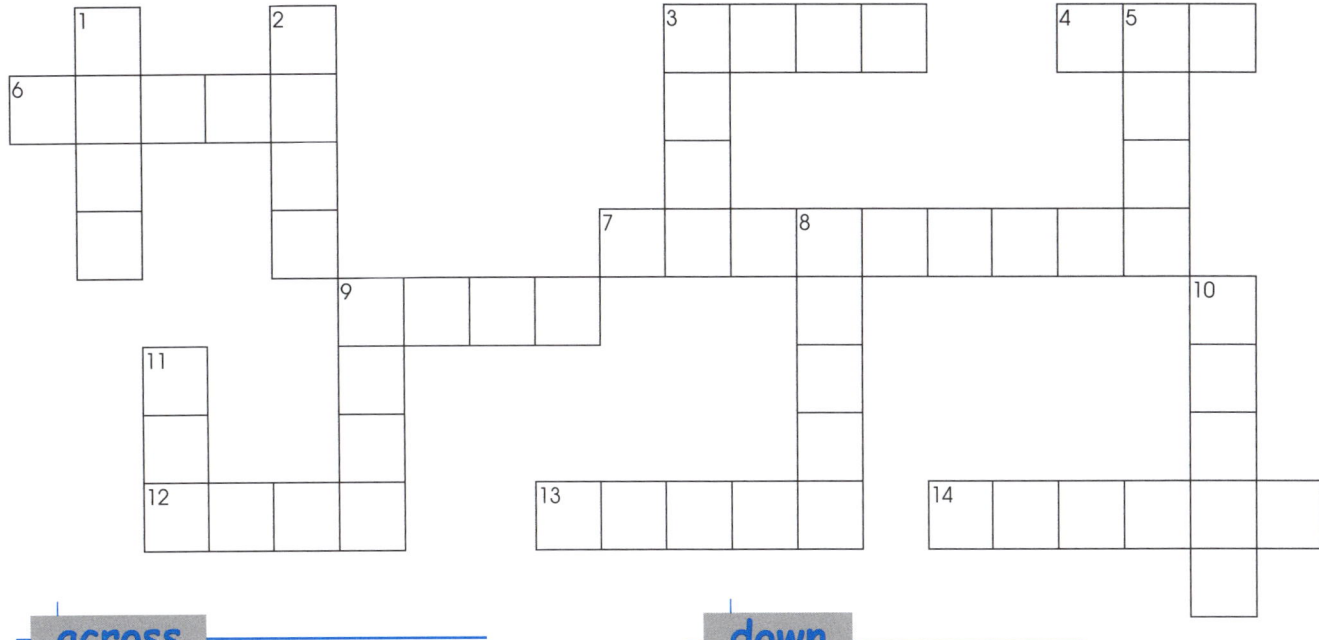

across

3. A mammal that lives in the ocean
4. A cove is a small _____
6. A line containing wires
7. The day before today
9. A feeling of danger or evil
12. Used to hold up trousers
13. Remember to _____ the plants with water
14. Information going out

down

1. Computer information
2. Opposite of fake
3. To rescue
5. Two children were _____ from school today
8. Between yesterday and tomorrow
9. The students _____ sick after eating too much
10. Information going in
11. You have a big _____ to do if you want to finish today

Alphabetical Order

4. Put these list words into alphabetical order.

cable   away   seal   input   spray   disc   real

Spelling Challenges

- Write the words using look, say, trace, cover, write, check.
- Write five more words that rhyme with 'bay'.
- Write the revision list in alphabetical order.

UNIT 1

Spelling Sums

5. (a) yes + ter + day = _____

    (b) to + day = _____

    (c) spr + ay = _____

    (d) a + way = _____

All Mixed Up

6. Unjumble these list words.

    (a) icsd _____ (b) yaspr _____

    (c) telf _____ (d) lear _____

    (e) yab _____ (f) adtoy _____

    (g) yaaw _____ (h) aatd _____

Synonyms

7. Find a list or revision word with a similar meaning.

    (a) work _____ (b) little _____

    (c) touched _____ (d) below _____

    (e) facts _____ (f) match _____

Missing Words

8. Complete, using one of these list words.

    | job | felt | away | save |

    (a) I will _____ for a new bike.

    (b) She was _____ because she had a cold.

    (c) The snake _____ cold.

    (d) It is your _____ to clean the board.

List
cable
data
input
job
output
disc
save
spray
belt
felt
seal
real
fear
bay
euro
today
yesterday
away

Revision
lump
go
sand
band
day
ant
side
till
thing
chin
game
under
car
leaf
small

UNIT 1

9. Find these list words in the word search.

cable   seal
data   real
input   fear
job   bay
output euro
disc   today
save   yesterday
spray   away
belt   felt

i	n	p	u	t	q	l	s	e	l	b	a	c
g	o	l	h	y	a	b	t	p	m	r	s	w
f	r	w	d	e	l	m	f	e	r	u	o	t
h	s	w	r	b	i	b	a	t	l	a	r	e
n	e	s	u	o	t	b	d	o	r	s	y	y
b	a	a	s	u	u	j	i	d	u	t	r	a
e	l	v	t	t	d	o	s	a	i	l	o	d
y	n	e	u	p	p	b	c	y	t	e	c	r
r	p	e	s	u	r	n	s	l	a	f	l	e
a	a	s	a	t	w	u	t	e	u	r	o	t
e	l	t	l	j	o	l	m	c	k	r	b	s
f	a	j	w	r	e	o	p	b	t	l	z	e
d	e	p	r	b	r	s	n	t	a	w	a	y

Memory Master

10. Cover the list words. Write two from memory.

_____ _____

Write a sentence using both words.

_____

_____

Word Worm

11. Circle each list word you can find in the word worm.

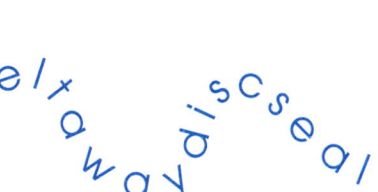

sprayeurodatasavebeltawaydiscseal

UNIT 2

List Words	Test 1	Test 2	Test 3	Test 4	Test 5	T
text						
boss						
lift						
screen						
strap						
pasta						
catch						
church						
club						
flat						
plan						
plant						
laser						
slept						
remote						
metre						
gram						
litre						

Look   Say   Trace   Cover   Write   Check

Difficult Words I Have Found	Test 1	Test 2	Test 3	T

What am I?

1. (a) I can be many different shapes.

   You boil me to make me soft.

   You eat me.

   I am _____

   (b) People sing in me.

   I have many windows.

   You come to me to pray.

   I am a _____

   (c) I need sunlight to grow.

   I can have flowers.

   I am green.

   I am a _____

2. Use list words to solve the crossword.

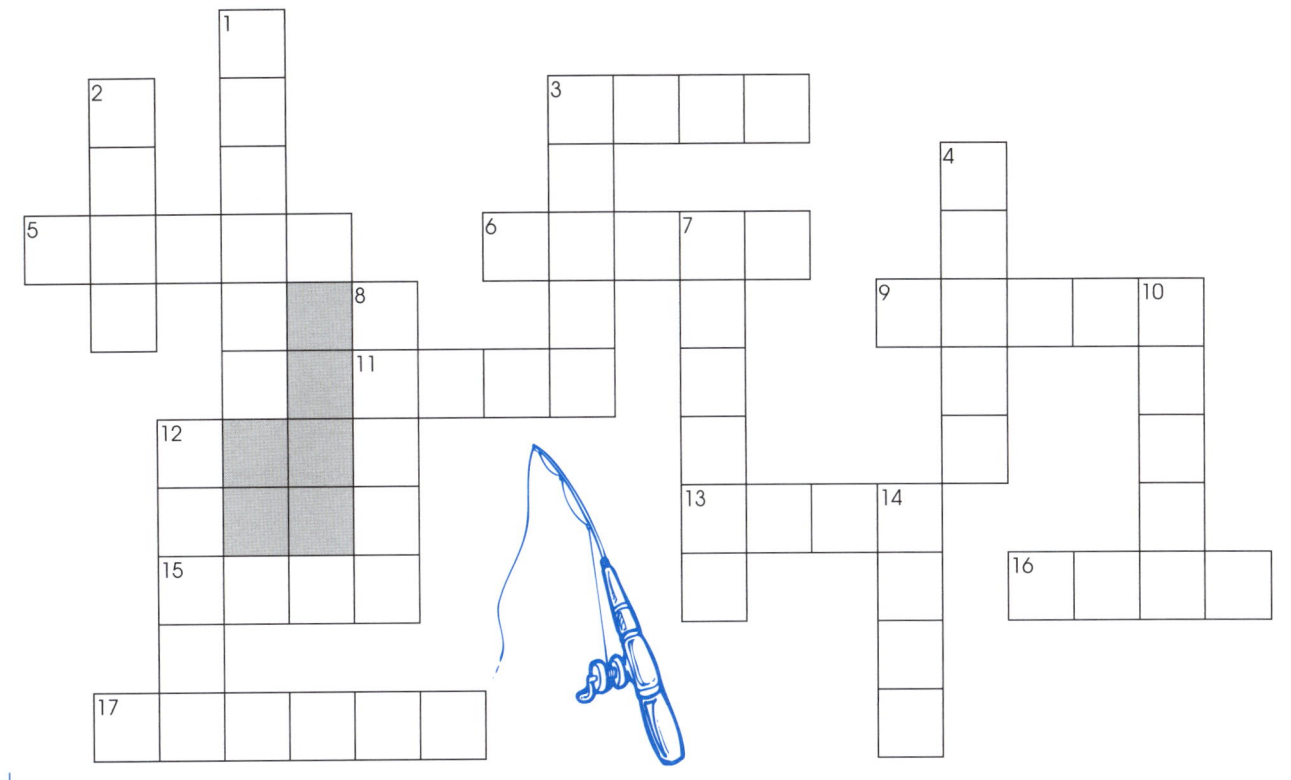

across

3. To prepare for something
5. A special type of light
6. You use a fishing line to _____ a fish
9. Used to hold things down
11. To pick something up
13. The school has a chess _____
15. The words of an author
16. Smooth or level
17. Far away

down

1. The front of the television
2. A unit of measure (mass)
3. To put into the ground
4. A unit of measure (volume)
7. A place of worship and prayer
8. Today I sleep, yesterday I _____
10. A food often used in Italian cooking
12. A unit of measure (length)
14. Leader (slang)

Missing Letters

3. (a) p___ ___t___ _____
   (b) ___ ___ur___ ___ _____
   (c) ___ ___s___r _____
   (d) m___ ___r___ _____
   (e) ___cr___ ___n _____

Spelling Challenges

- Write the words using look, say, trace, cover, write, check.
- Write five more words that start with 'pl'.
- Choose five revision words and write a sentence for each.

UNIT 2

Rhyming Words

4. Choose a rhyming word from your list.

   (a) hat _____

   (b) batch _____

   (c) flap _____

   (d) seen _____

Word Meanings

5. Match each word to its meaning.

   (a) flat   •   • a place of worship

   (b) lift   •   • to get hold of

   (c) church •   • even

   (d) catch   •   • to raise up

Antonyms

6. Find a list word or revision word with the opposite meaning.

   (a) drop _____ (b) hilly _____

   (c) took _____ (d) bold _____

   (e) lower _____ (f) subtract _____

Same Sound

7. Circle the correct word.

   (a) Can you (sea/see) the screen?

   (b) It will be sunny this (week/weak).

List
text
boss
lift
screen
strap
pasta
catch
church
club
flat
plan
plant
laser
slept
remote
metre
gram
litre

Revision
jump
pram
add
truck
week
disk
nine
will
swing
much
gave
saw
star
sea
shy

My Spelling Workbook Book C | 8 | www.prim-ed.com | Prim-Ed Publishing

UNIT 2

8. Find these list words in the word search.

text   plan
boss   plant
lift   laser
screen   slept
strap   remote
pasta   metre
catch   gram
church   litre
club   flat

s	c	r	e	e	n	i	p	t	g	r	o	l
v	x	b	i	b	u	l	c	j	r	l	a	i
d	n	t	r	l	i	t	r	e	a	a	t	f
w	n	x	r	e	s	a	l	p	m	n	a	t
p	i	e	b	f	t	w	a	r	l	i	p	o
c	f	t	i	t	r	r	e	t	o	m	e	r
h	s	q	m	n	t	a	j	q	r	s	l	t
u	l	f	l	s	e	n	b	h	c	t	a	c
r	e	p	j	p	a	e	a	q	h	e	s	p
c	p	l	a	r	t	d	w	l	n	r	u	s
h	t	a	u	s	m	b	o	n	p	t	v	s
d	w	n	p	r	t	s	l	m	r	e	u	o
f	l	a	t	r	o	a	t	l	e	m	i	b

Letters into Words

9. Write four list words using the letters in the screen.

a u l
f c   t
n p b

Secret Words

10. (a) Take 'c' off catch and put in 'm'. _____

(b) Take 'b' off boss and put in 'cr'. _____

(c) Take 'tr' off strap and put in 'n'. _____

(d) Add 'e' to plan. _____

(e) Take 'g' of gram and put in 'p'. _____

UNIT 3

List Words	Test 1	Test 2	Test 3	Test 4	Test 5	T
there						
flip						
flower						
song						
soft						
format						
solid						
blank						
bank						
drank						
thank						
because						
began						
begin						
before						
behind						
your						
hear						

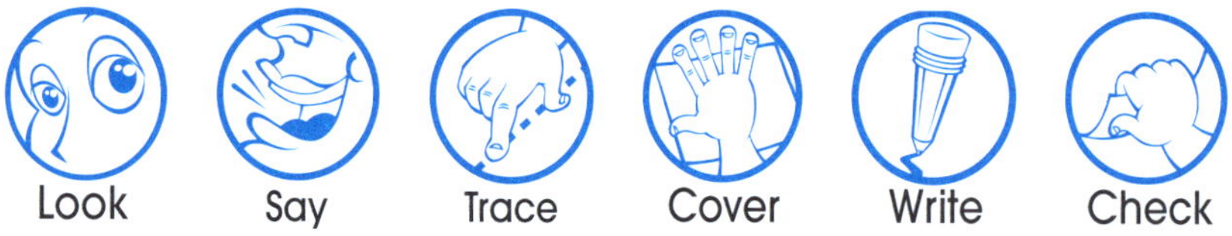

Look Say Trace Cover Write Check

Difficult Words I Have Found	Test 1	Test 2	Test 3	T

Spelling Sums

1. (a) be + cause = __because__

    (b) so + lid = _____

    (c) be + gan = _____

    (d) be + fore = _____

    (e) bl + ank = _____

    (f) for + mat = _____

    (g) be + hind = _____

    (h) dr + ank = _____

UNIT 3

2. Use list words to solve the crossword.

across

1. Opposite of hard
4. The class sang a _____
5. At the back of
6. Hard
7. The ball is over _____
8. I can't come to play _____ I have to do my homework
9. Is that _____ dog?
10. The band will _____ to play
11. To turn over quickly
12. A place where large amounts of money are kept
13. Did you _____ the thunder?
14. All the runners _____ a lot of water
15. _____ you!

down

2. The rose had only one red _____
3. Opposite of after
8. Everyone ran inside after it _____ to rain
11. The way something is put together.
12. The page was _____

Small Words

3. Find small words in these list words.

(a) song _____
(b) bank _____
(c) begin _____
(d) your _____
(e) hear _____
(f) format _____

Spelling Challenges

- Write the words using look, say, trace, cover, write, check.
- Write the revision list in alphabetical order.
- Write three more words that begin with 'dr'.

UNIT 3

Mixed up Sentences

4. (a) blank. is paper The

   _____

   (b) computer the disk. Format

   _____

   (c) The solid. shape is

   _____

All Mixed Up

5. Unjumble the words.

   (a) nogs _____   (b) kabn _____

   (c) oruy _____   (d) enagb _____

   (e) inhebd _____   (f) pilf _____

Missing Words

6. Complete using one of these list words.

   | before | soft | flower | hear |

   (a) The bee landed on the _____.

   (b) Read me a story _____ I go to sleep.

   (c) I can _____ you from outside.

   (d) The puppy felt warm and _____.

Same Sound

7. Circle the correct word.

   (a) The girls put (there, they're, their) bikes over (there, they're, their.)

   (b) '(Your, You're) going to pick up (your, you're) books,' said the teacher.

List
there
flip
flower
song
soft
format
solid
blank
bank
drank
thank
because
began
begin
before
behind
your
hear

Revision
stamp
from
hand
clock
year
milk
five
have
sing
rich
came
ever
arm
tea
dry

My Spelling Workbook Book C • 12 • www.prim-ed.com • Prim-Ed Publishing

UNIT 3

8. Find these list words in the word search.

there   thank
flip   because
flower began
song   begin
soft   before
format behind
solid   your
blank   hear
bank   drank

e	p	l	i	k	n	a	l	b	t	r	e	s
r	k	t	u	y	o	u	r	b	j	l	g	o
e	o	n	p	i	l	b	e	g	a	n	t	n
h	i	v	a	g	l	e	u	t	r	y	n	g
t	b	p	o	r	e	m	d	n	i	h	e	b
s	l	e	r	n	d	s	o	l	i	d	e	f
h	o	n	g	r	i	b	f	k	l	t	r	o
e	x	f	j	i	d	a	p	n	m	p	o	r
a	q	r	t	u	n	n	d	a	r	t	f	m
r	a	b	o	t	s	k	r	h	p	l	e	a
e	s	u	a	c	e	b	n	t	r	o	b	t
g	u	e	l	s	n	o	p	q	r	n	l	p
p	i	l	f	r	l	b	f	l	o	w	e	r

Memory Master

9. Cover the list words. Write two from memory.
   _____ _____

   Write a sentence using both words.
   _____

Word Hunt

10. (a) Which list words begin with 'b'? _____ _____
    _____ _____ _____ _____

    (b) Which list words rhyme with sank?
    _____ _____ _____

    (c) Which list or revision words have 'ear' in them?
    _____ _____

    (d) Which list words have **more than** five letters?
    _____ _____ _____ _____

Prim-Ed Publishing   www.prim-ed.com   13   My Spelling Workbook Book C

UNIT 4

List Words	Test 1	Test 2	Test 3	Test 4	Test 5	T
face						
race						
place						
made						
age						
cage						
sale						
tale						
cave						
cork						
fort						
horse						
horn						
wore						
birthday						
kept						
month						
tear						

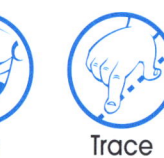

Look   Say   Trace   Cover   Write   Check

Difficult Words I Have Found	Test 1	Test 2	Test 3	T

Word Worm

1. Circle and write each list word found in the word worm.

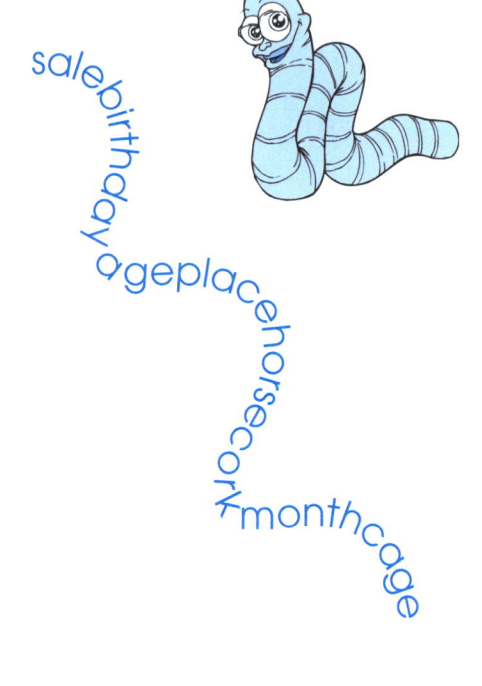

salebirthdayageplacehorsecorkmonthcage

_____
_____
_____
_____
_____
_____
_____

My Spelling Workbook Book C

UNIT 4

2. Use list words to solve the crossword.

across

4. Happy _____
5. Put in the top of bottles
6. The cars had a _____ around the track
8. Money is _____ in a bank
10. To keep things tidy, everything needs to have its own _____
11. Something pet birds are kept in
13. 'For _____', said the sign
15. A large animal
16. To rip
17. January is a _____ of the year

down

1. A place where soldiers live
2. Part of your body
3. She _____ a red dress to the party
7. How old you are
9. I _____ a cake yesterday
11. A natural hole under the ground
12. A story
14. Found on a car for warning people

Synonyms

3. Find a list word or revision word with a similar meaning.

(a) rip _____
(b) leak _____
(c) story _____
(d) table _____

Spelling Challenges

• Write the words using look, say, trace, cover, write, check.
• Choose five revision words and write a sentence for each.
• Write three more words that rhyme with 'meat'.

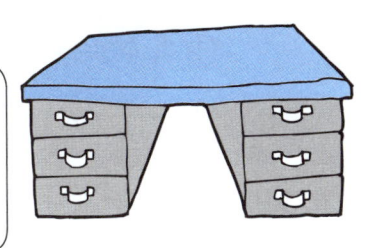

Prim-Ed Publishing   www.prim-ed.com   15   My Spelling Workbook Book C

UNIT 4

Missing Letters

4. (a) ___g___ _____

   (b) h___ ___ ___e _____

   (c) ___l___c___ _____

   (d) f___ ___t _____

   (e) ___on___ ___ _____

Word Meanings

5. Match each word to its meaning.

   (a) to rip • • horse

   (b) an animal • • race

   (c) animals and birds are kept in this • • tear

   (d) a chase or competition • • cage

Alphabetical Order

6. Put these words into alphabetical order.

   > horse kept cave age cork wore face made

   _____

   _____

Same Sound

7. Circle the correct word.

   (a) The (maid, made) came to the house and (made, maid) the beds.

   (b) The (tale, tail) told by the boy was about a mouse's (tail, tale).

   (c) He had (been, bean) to the circus before.

   (d) In the (war, wore) the soldiers (wore, war) uniforms.

List

face
race
place
made
age
cage
sale
tale
cave
cork
fort
horse
horn
wore
birthday
kept
month
tear

Revision

end
drip
and
black
wool
desk
ride
been
such
name
never
farm
meat
try

UNIT 4

8. Find these list words in the word search.

face	fort
race	horse
place	horn
made	wore
age	birthday
cage	kept
sale	tale
cave	cork
month	tear

m	i	e	r	n	w	l	a	p	l	a	c	e
a	n	g	b	l	o	g	j	r	a	e	t	o
d	e	a	j	o	r	p	z	l	o	e	j	t
e	w	c	r	a	e	d	e	s	r	o	h	n
j	t	i	n	o	y	a	d	h	t	r	i	b
h	o	r	n	d	t	a	l	e	f	x	o	c
b	r	a	j	t	l	e	f	h	v	r	a	a
a	p	t	o	r	i	k	o	k	j	u	l	v
b	g	n	i	o	t	r	e	p	r	u	z	e
e	l	e	m	f	y	x	l	p	b	o	t	c
c	r	m	o	n	t	h	j	d	t	r	c	l
a	b	e	r	l	i	r	i	p	o	m	u	p
f	i	e	l	a	s	t	o	i	e	c	a	r

Shape Sorter

9. Write the word that fits in each shape.

   (a) 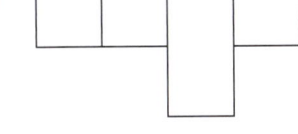
   (b) 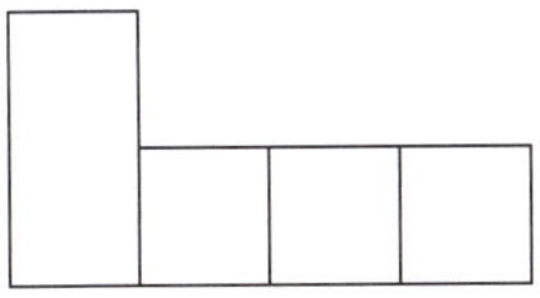
   (c) 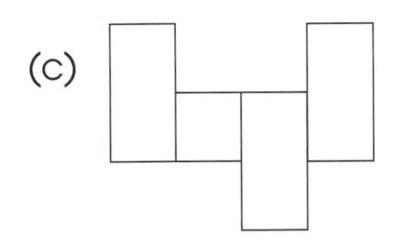
   (d)

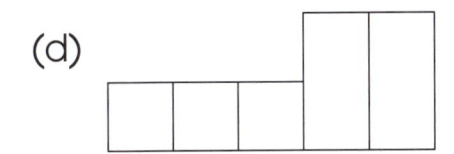

Similar Patterns

10. face   sale   age

What is the same about these words?
_____

Find the other list or revision words with the same rule.
_____
_____

UNIT 5

List Words	Test 1	Test 2	Test 3	Test 4	Test 5	T
held						
hunt						
icon						
broke						
woke						
insert						
stone						
mobile						
delete						
chose						
close						
those						
second						
minute						
hose						
scroll						
email						
house						

Look Say Trace Cover Write Check

Difficult Words I Have Found	Test 1	Test 2	Test 3	T

Short Words

1. Match these words to their abbreviations.

    (a) minute • • a.m.

    (b) second • • min.

    (c) afternoon • • p.m.

    (d) morning • • sec.

Small Words

2. Find small words in these list words.

    (a) delete

    _____

    (b) scroll

    _____

    (c) second

    _____

    (d) email

    _____

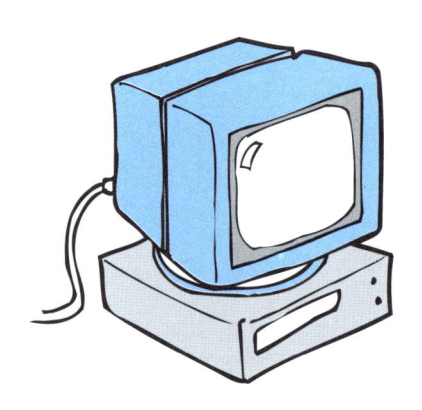

My Spelling Workbook Book C

UNIT 5

3. Use list words to solve the crossword.

across

2. To get rid of something on a computer screen
4. He _____ up at 6 o'clock
7. To move down or up a computer screen
8. The accident _____ up the traffic
9. She rang on her _____ phone
11. A smooth rock
12. The teacher _____ me to clean the board
13. To put something into
14. Used to transport water

down

1. The glass _____ when it was dropped
3. A way to send messages by computer
5. To shut something
6. After first
8. To look for
9. 60 seconds equal one _____
10. A place where people live

Changing Words

4. Change one letter from each word to make a list word.

   (a) store → _____

   (b) nose → _____

   (c) mouse → _____

   (d) head → _____

Spelling Challenges

- Write the words using look, say, trace, cover, write, check.
- Write the revision words in alphabetical order.
- Find other words that have abbreviations.

UNIT 5

All Mixed Up

5. Unjumble the list words.

   (a) thnu _____ (b) ledh _____

   (c) korbe _____ (d) iocn _____

   (e) seohu _____ (f) kowe _____

   (g) emolib _____ (h) tseno _____

Antonyms

6. Find a list or revision word with the opposite meaning.

   (a) slept _____ (b) open _____

   (c) dislike _____ (d) short _____

   (e) soft _____ (f) include _____

Missing Words

7. Complete using one of these list words.

   | held | delete | chose | hose | second |

   (a) Go to the garden and turn on the _____.

   (b) The girl _____ her doll tightly.

   (c) _____ the sentence from your work.

   (d) He _____ the red ball from the basket.

   (e) It was the _____ time the dog had been lost.

List
held
hunt
icon
broke
woke
insert
stone
mobile
delete
chose
close
those
second
minute
hose
scroll
email
house

Revision
pump
so
drum
lick
wood
pole
like
tree
long
punch
ate
make
hard
seat
fly

UNIT 5

8. Find these list words in the word search.

held   close

hunt   those

icon   second

broke   minute

woke   hose

insert   scroll

stone   email

mobile   house

delete   chose

d	h	o	u	s	e	s	p	l	h	o	p	e
l	r	d	o	e	e	o	e	e	d	e	r	n
e	m	e	l	t	r	p	p	c	s	l	i	m
h	a	l	a	u	i	e	r	n	o	o	j	t
t	h	e	e	n	e	s	o	h	t	n	h	l
a	h	t	s	i	g	r	u	m	n	i	d	c
b	o	e	o	m	e	m	a	i	l	f	j	c
o	s	u	l	k	r	l	l	o	r	c	s	c
w	e	r	c	t	o	p	e	n	t	r	u	b
z	o	l	b	r	e	n	o	t	s	g	n	r
j	u	k	t	i	n	s	e	r	t	l	o	o
t	i	k	e	r	o	t	i	l	l	a	c	k
t	n	u	h	e	l	i	b	o	m	r	i	e

Letters into Words

9. Write five list words using the letters in the water.

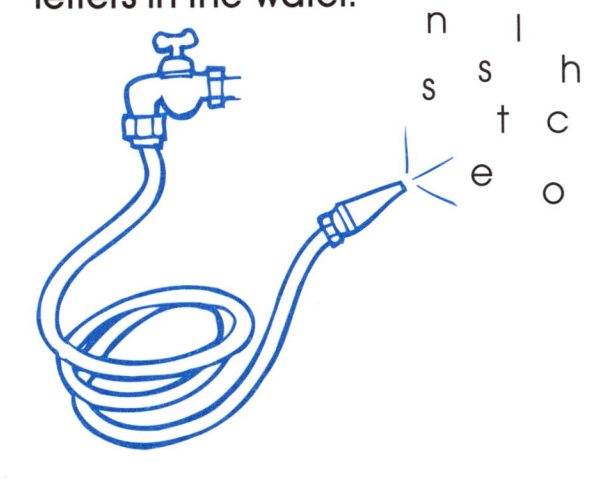

n   l
s   s   h
    t   c
    e   o

_____ _____

_____ _____

_____

Memory Master

10. Cover the list words. Write two from memory.

_____

_____

Write a sentence using both words.

_____

_____

_____

_____

UNIT 6

List Words	Test 1	Test 2	Test 3	Test 4	Test 5	T
ice						
nice						
slice						
wife						
life						
hike						
mile						
while						
time						
fire						
bite						
site						
white						
water						
afraid						
again						
mail						
paint						

Look Say Trace Cover Write Check

Difficult Words I Have Found	Test 1	Test 2	Test 3	T

Spelling Sums

1. (a) a + gain = _____

   (b) h + ike = _____

   (c) m + ile = _____

   (d) n + ice = _____

   (e) a + fraid = _____

   (f) f + ire = _____

Rhyming Words

2. Choose a rhyming word from your list.

   (a) tail _____

   (b) lime _____

   (c) tyre _____

   (d) like _____

   (e) made _____

   (f) saint _____

My Spelling Workbook Book C 22 www.prim-ed.com Prim-Ed Publishing

UNIT 6

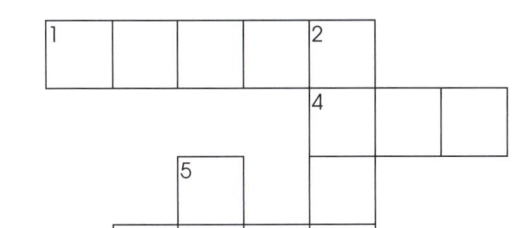

3. Use list words to solve the crossword.

down

2. Pleasant
3. May I have a cold drink of _____?
5. It gave me the fright of my _____
6. To cut into thin pieces
8. To send by post
9. A measure of distance
12. Something your teeth do
14. A place
15. Opposite to black
16. What _____ is the bus arriving?

across

1. You will need to try it _____ if you want to get it right
4. Would you like _____ with your drink?
7. Husband and _____
10. To be frightened
11. A long walk, usually in the country
13. This is very hot
15. Can you wait for a _____?
17. Comes in many different colours

Spelling Challenges

- Write the words using look, say, trace, cover, write, check.
- Find other words with the pattern 'ai'. For example, r**ai**n and b**ai**t.
- Choose 'g' words from your revision list and put them in a sentence.

What am I?

4. I am cold.
   I can melt.
   I keep your drink cool.
   I am _____

UNIT 6

Secret Words

List: ice, nice, slice, wife, life, hike, mile, while, time, fire, bite, site, white, water, afraid, again, mail, paint

5. (a) Take 'm' off mail and put in 'sn'. _____

   (b) Take 'b' off bite and put in 'k'. _____

   (c) Take 'h' off hike and put in 'b'. _____

   (d) Take 'n' off nice and put in 'tw'. _____

   (e) Take 'f' off fire and add 'w'. _____

   (f) Add 'st' to the end of again. _____

Antonyms

6. Find a list or revision word with the opposite meaning.

   (a) black _____   (b) unafraid _____

   (c) bad _____   (d) dirty _____

   (e) husband _____   (f) near _____

Synonyms

Revision: camp, flag, land, duck, good, hole, line, green, bang, lunch, gate, live, far, clean, each

7. Find a list or revision word with a similar meaning.

   (a) cut _____

   (b) walk _____

   (c) scared _____

   (d) chew _____

   (e) great _____

   (f) ground _____

My Spelling Workbook Book C

UNIT 6

8. Find these list words in the word search.

ice bite
nice site
slice white
wife water
life afraid
hike again
mile mail
while paint
time fire

p	i	r	t	d	e	e	t	i	s	e	e	k
r	w	h	i	l	e	b	a	o	r	l	k	i
w	i	s	p	a	l	i	a	m	t	t	i	c
a	v	a	a	j	n	i	n	e	r	t	h	k
t	e	i	i	e	r	t	e	m	o	l	i	k
e	t	e	n	p	w	h	i	t	e	l	r	t
r	i	o	t	e	r	g	f	t	o	p	x	i
s	b	h	d	l	o	g	u	i	t	u	c	m
e	o	i	a	i	i	e	b	t	r	e	n	e
p	l	w	r	s	a	f	u	l	d	e	i	m
e	v	i	e	v	n	r	e	c	i	n	a	a
c	i	f	m	a	k	t	f	e	o	m	g	m
k	l	e	s	l	i	c	e	a	m	t	a	k

Alphabetical Order

9. Write these words in alphabetical order.

paint bite wife site ice while afraid time

_____

_____

Secret Code

10. Use the secret code to find out the list or revision word.

| 1 | 2 | 3 | 4 | 5 | 6 | 7 | 8 | 9 | 10 | 11 | 12 |
| A | B | C | E | F | G | H | I | N | R | T | W |

(a) ___ ___ ___ ___ ___
     12 7   8 11   4

(b) ___ ___ ___ ___ ___
     12 1 11   4 10

(c) ___ ___ ___ ___ ___
      6 10 4   4   9

(d) ___ ___ ___
      8   3   4

(e) ___ ___ ___ ___
      5   8 10   4

(f) ___ ___ ___ ___ ___
      1   6   1   8   9

UNIT 7

List Words	Test 1	Test 2	Test 3	Test 4	Test 5	T
crop						
trip						
stuck						
kick						
deck						
skip						
skin						
done						
love						
skate						
egg						
peanut						
crisp						
chip						
table						
little						
apple						
salad						

Look   Say   Trace   Cover   Write   Check

Difficult Words I Have Found	Test 1	Test 2	Test 3	T

Word Hunt

1. (a) Which list words start with 'sk'?

   _____
   _____
   _____

   (b) Which list words end in 'le'?

   _____
   _____
   _____

What am I?

2. I am small and rounded.

   I am yummy for breakfast.

   Birds and reptiles hatch out of me.

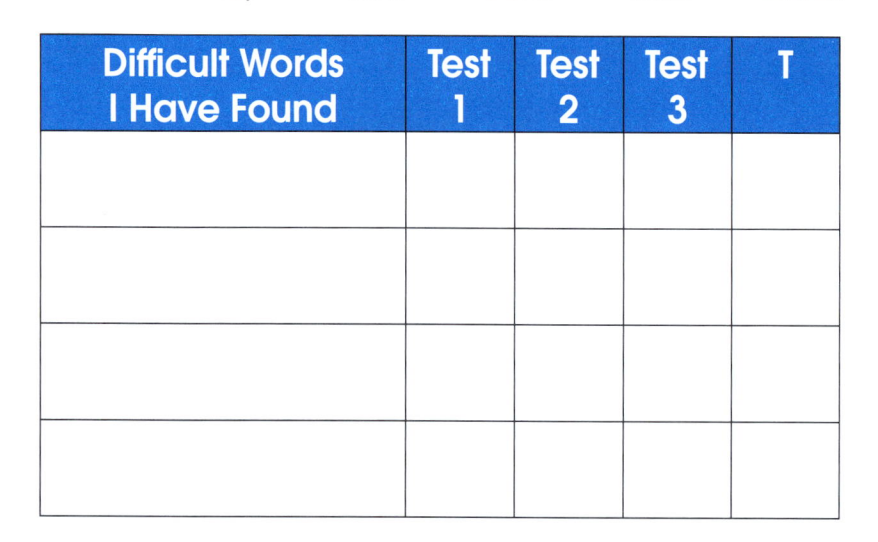

   I am an _____

My Spelling Workbook Book C — 26 — www.prim-ed.com   Prim-Ed Publishing

UNIT 7

3. Use list words to solve the crossword.

across

4. Have you _____ your homework?
5. To jump from one foot to the other
8. To move across ice
9. He ate a hot _____
10. The car was _____ in the mud
12. The bird hatched from the _____
13. A small nut in a shell
14. Opposite to big
16. The name for a collection of cold vegetables

down

1. It was _____ at first sight!
2. The 'floor' in a ship
3. A 'Granny Smith' is one of these
6. Done with your foot
7. The lettuce was very _____
8. Your body is covered with _____
9. The _____ was harvested
11. Similar to 'voyage'
15. A _____ and chair

Small Words

4. Find a small word in these list words.

   (a) trip _____   (b) done _____

   (c) skate _____ (d) chip _____

   (e) skin _____   (f) peanut _____

Spelling Challenges

- Write the words using look, say, trace, cover, write, check.
- Write the revision list in alphabetical order.
- Choose five list words and write a sentence for each.

UNIT 7

All Mixed Up

5. (a) cikk _____ (b) dslaa _____

   (c) nedo _____ (d) geg _____

   (e) pihc _____ (f) ovel _____

   (g) titell _____ (h) isnk _____

Compound Words

6. Match the words to make a compound word.

   (a) skate •   • cloth

   (b) table •   • cup

   (c) egg •   • board

Synonyms

7. Find a list or revision word with a similar meaning.

   (a) small _____

   (b) finished _____

   (c) journey _____

   (d) desk _____

   (e) mail _____

   (f) begin _____

Word Worm

8. Circle and write the list words found in the word worm.

   _____
   _____
   _____
   _____
   _____
   _____
   _____

List
crop
trip
stuck
kick
deck
skip
skin
done
love
skate
egg
peanut
crisp
chip
table
little
apple
salad

Revision
send
slip
rock
rest
mole
hide
sleep
sang
chick
take
spoon
start
eat
all
teach

crispapplelittlelovecroptripegg

My Spelling Workbook Book C — www.prim-ed.com — Prim-Ed Publishing

UNIT 7

9. Find these list words in the word search.

stuck	skin
kick	crop
little	trip
deck	skip
done	love
share	egg
peanut	chip
crisp	table
salad	apple

p	i	r	t	t	r	a	w	l	h	e	i	k
i	s	a	l	a	d	b	a	o	o	l	d	i
r	p	e	a	n	u	t	c	v	m	t	e	c
o	t	o	l	i	m	i	r	e	h	t	i	k
a	h	n	n	i	k	s	i	o	r	i	b	t
d	g	e	l	p	p	a	s	l	t	l	y	o
m	d	o	n	e	d	g	p	n	i	g	m	t
s	r	h	i	t	r	g	i	s	t	u	c	k
v	h	t	o	n	a	e	m	i	p	i	h	c
p	l	a	o	e	p	b	l	o	d	a	e	t
o	a	m	r	v	i	g	l	r	w	e	s	h
r	o	p	r	e	k	i	a	e	o	t	c	e
c	r	a	w	h	s	l	g	o	n	t	g	k

Memory Master

10. Cover the list words. Write two from memory.

_____   _____

Write an interesting sentence using both words.

_____

_____

Read and Draw

11. (a) A girl on skates eating chips. (b) A boy on a table juggling eggs.

UNIT 8

List Words	Test 1	Test 2	Test 3	Test 4	Test 5	T
bigger						
high						
fight						
light						
might						
right						
night						
please						
leave						
around						
loud						
blow						
mow						
window						
yellow						
tomorrow						
own						
crow						

Look   Say   Trace   Cover   Write   Check

Difficult Words I Have Found	Test 1	Test 2	Test 3	T

Letters into Words

1. Write four list words using the letters in the window.

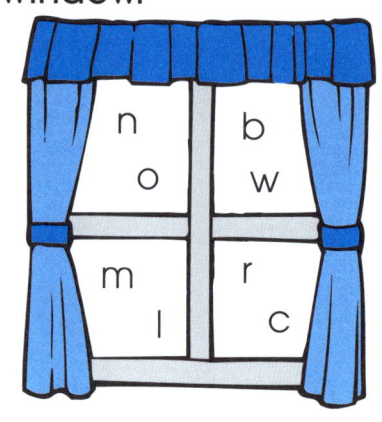

   n b
   o w
   m r
   l c

   _____
   _____
   _____
   _____

Word Challenge

2. Make as many little words as you can from the word in the box. You can rearrange the letters if you like.

   tonight

   _____
   _____
   _____
   _____
   _____

My Spelling Workbook Book C   30   www.prim-ed.com   Prim-Ed Publishing

3. Use list words to solve the crossword.

across

1. The colour of gold
4. The music was very _____
8. Larger
10. The wind was going to _____
12. Opposite of heavy
13. I will _____ the lawn
14. A word used with good manners
16. The cat chased the mouse _____
17. Opposite of left

down

2. Something you look through
3. The day after today
5. Opposite of low
6. A bird
7. To battle against
9. To go away
11. She _____ be back later
15. Opposite of day

Spelling Challenges

- Write the words using look, say, trace, cover, write, check.
- Write five more words that have 'ow' in them.
- Choose five revision words and write a sentence for each.

UNIT 8

Missing Words

List

bigger
high
fight
light
might
right
night
please
leave
around
loud
blow
mow
window
yellow
tomorrow
own
crow

4. Complete using one of these list words.

   blow   Tomorrow   around   bigger   right

   (a) _____ is my birthday!

   (b) Can you _____ up the balloon?

   (c) My dog is _____ than my cat.

   (d) Walk _____ the flowers, not over them.

   (e) Are you left-handed or _____-handed?

Antonyms

5. Find a list or revision word with the opposite meaning.

   (a) smaller _____ (b) low _____

   (c) heavy _____ (d) wrong _____

   (e) straight _____ (f) came _____

   (g) in _____ (h) sleep _____

Synonyms

Revision

bend
out
neck
pest
sole
went
street
hang
miss
wake
tooth
bone
read
ball
beach

6. Find a list or revision word with a similar meaning.

   (a) brawl _____ (b) drape _____

   (c) noisy _____ (d) cut _____

Same Sound

7. Circle the correct word.

   (a) 'What (right, write,) have you to (right, write,) about that now?' asked the teacher.

   (b) '(Hi, high),' said Mum. 'How (high, hi) can you jump?'

UNIT 8

8. Find these list words in the word search.

bigger	around
high	loud
fight	blow
light	mow
might	window
right	yellow
night	tomorrow
own	please
crow	leave

b	e	l	d	t	o	u	l	t	h	g	i	f
i	n	t	o	h	o	p	f	l	o	u	d	r
g	a	b	j	g	r	w	e	u	i	h	u	n
g	t	l	l	i	b	i	n	t	h	g	i	r
e	h	o	a	m	d	n	u	o	r	a	b	l
r	g	w	r	e	t	d	w	l	o	t	i	g
m	c	g	p	l	a	o	p	n	i	g	h	t
e	r	h	l	o	r	w	i	l	n	t	r	s
v	o	t	o	r	u	t	m	n	e	l	z	u
a	w	r	o	u	h	h	w	o	r	a	b	l
e	a	m	r	o	l	g	u	t	w	o	s	b
l	o	k	r	t	m	i	l	o	d	a	s	e
t	r	e	w	o	l	l	e	y	h	i	g	h

Alphabetical Order

9. Write these words in alphabetical order.

| window | high | tomorrow | loud | yellow | light | own | bigger |

(a) _____   (b) _____

(c) _____   (d) _____

(e) _____   (f) _____

(g) _____   (h) _____

Word Meanings

10. Match each word to its meaning.

(a) yellow   •   • a bird

(b) leave   •   • a battle

(c) fight   •   • a colour

(d) crow   •   • to exit

UNIT 9

List Words	Test 1	Test 2	Test 3	Test 4	Test 5	T
four						
frog						
cent						
yell						
spring						
use						
other						
another						
brother						
mother						
cover						
front						
son						
nothing						
die						
lie						
tie						
toe						

Look   Say   Trace   Cover   Write   Check

Difficult Words I Have Found	Test 1	Test 2	Test 3	T

What am I?

1. (a) I have a nail.

   I come in groups of ten.

   I am a

   _____

   (b) I can be any age.

   I have many names.

   My siblings call me their b_____.

   I am a

   _____

   (c) I swim and jump.

   I eat flies.

   I begin life as a tadpole.

   I am a

   _____

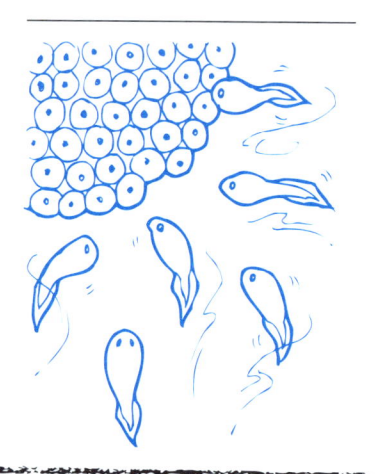

My Spelling Workbook Book C

UNIT 9

2. Use list words to solve the crossword.

across

4. An untruth
6. _____ and sister
9. Scream
10. Part of your foot
11. Half of eight
13. Can you see across to the _____ side of the river?
15. Can you _____ your shoe laces?
16. A season
17. Daughter and _____

down

1. Father and _____
2. To stop living
3. Tomorrow is _____ day
5. Opposite of back
7. _____ your mouth when you cough
8. Dollar and _____
11. An animal that jumps
12. Not anything
14. May I _____ your new pencil?

Spelling Challenges

- Write the words using look, say, trace, cover, write, check.
- Write five more words that end in 'er'.
- Write the revision list in alphabetical order.

Adding Endings

3. Add 'ing' to these words.

List Word	Add 'ing'
(a) tie	tying
(b) die	
(c) lie	

What is the rule?

If you add 'ing' to a word ending in 'ie', you

_____

_____

Prim-Ed Publishing   www.prim-ed.com   35   My Spelling Workbook Book C

UNIT 9

All Mixed Up

List
four
frog
cent
yell
spring
use
other
another
brother
mother
cover
front
son
nothing
die
lie
tie
toe

4. Unjumble the list words.

   (a) tenc _____ (b) ufro _____

   (c) eit _____ (d) orgf _____

   (e) ide _____ (f) leyl _____

   (g) vecro _____ (h) tohrean _____

Shape Sorter

5. Write a list word that fits in each shape.

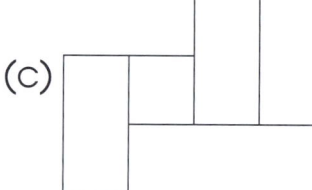

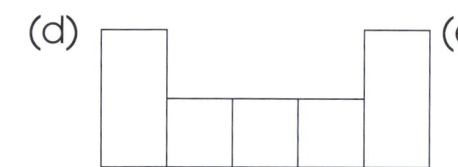

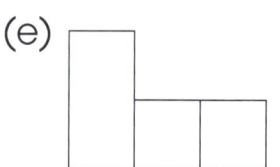

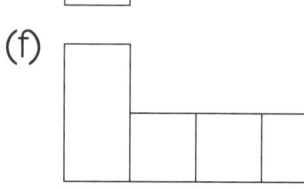

   (a) (b) (c)

   (d) (e) (f)

Changing Words

6. Change one letter from each word to make a list word.

   (a) won → _____ (b) fell → _____

   (c) rent → _____ (d) from → _____

   (e) did → _____ (f) top → _____

Same Sound

7. Circle the correct word.

   (a) The (for, four) girls ran (four, for) the blue team in the race.

   (b) The messenger (sent, cent, scent) his (son, sun) to the bank.

Revision
grow
swim
nest
kite
sweep
chop
zoo
mean
coat
tray
old
town
thin
shot
mill

UNIT 9

8. Find these list words in the word search.

four	cover
frog	front
cent	son
yell	nothing
spring	die
use	lie
other	tie
another	toe
brother	mother

g	t	n	o	r	f	a	e	i	e	s	l	e
o	c	e	n	t	r	a	b	s	s	o	p	i
a	l	d	e	o	t	u	m	n	u	c	n	l
s	o	n	r	v	l	o	p	t	z	q	o	y
b	i	l	d	u	t	e	e	r	e	h	t	o
a	n	o	t	h	e	r	p	l	y	s	h	m
w	e	c	e	t	b	u	r	a	b	l	i	f
s	t	r	y	d	o	b	e	l	r	i	n	o
o	p	t	x	m	i	l	v	g	o	r	g	t
y	o	r	n	t	i	e	o	d	t	o	a	r
e	l	u	i	r	e	n	c	o	h	u	r	u
l	e	o	p	n	t	l	i	b	e	s	g	o
l	t	r	i	g	g	o	r	f	r	t	u	f

Word Hunt

9. (a) Which list words end with 'er'?

_____

_____

_____

_____

(b) Which list words rhyme with 'my'?

_____

_____

(c) Which revision word means the same as 'nasty'?

_____

Word Worm

10. Circle and list each word found in the word worm.

toefrogmotherdieyellcent

_____

_____

_____

_____

_____

_____

UNIT 10

List Words	Test 1	Test 2	Test 3	Test 4	Test 5	T
sister						
letter						
better						
butter						
dinner						
child						
fast						
last						
past						
glass						
class						
grass						
ask						
bath						
after						
afternoon						
father						
our						

Look Say Trace Cover Write Check

Difficult Words I Have Found	Test 1	Test 2	Test 3	T

Small Words

1. Find a small word in these list words.

   (a) ask

   _____

   (b) bath

   _____

   (c) father

   _____

   (d) dinner

   _____

What am I?

2. I am yellow.

   I come from a cow.

   You spread me on bread.

   I am

   _____

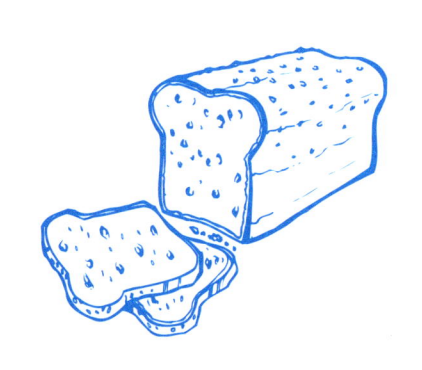

My Spelling Workbook Book C — www.prim-ed.com Prim-Ed Publishing

UNIT 10

3. Use list words to solve the crossword.

across

4. Opposite to before
5. May I have a _____ of water?
10. Found in most gardens
12. You can do _____ if you train harder
14. Can be filled with water
16. Brother and _____
17. Opposite of first

down

1. A group of students
2. Opposite of mother
3. Belonging to us
6. The time after morning
7. The evening meal
8. Opposite of slow
9. To put a question to someone
11. A written message
13. A young person
14. Put on bread
15. Opposite of future

Spelling Challenges

- Write the words using look, say, trace, cover, write, check.
- Write five more words that end in 'er'.
- Choose five list words and write a sentence for each.

Missing Letters

4. (a) f ___ ___ t _____
   (b) ___ sk _____
   (c) g___a___s _____
   (d) ___ ___il___ _____
   (e) p___s___ _____
   (f) ___ft___ ___oo___ _____

UNIT 10

Missing Words

5. Complete, using one of these list words.

   | afternoon   grass   past   fast   sister   bath |

   (a) My _____ is two years older than I.

   (b) We will play sport in the _____.

   (c) You can have a _____ or a shower.

   (d) The _____ by the road is turning brown.

   (e) How _____ can you run?

   (f) The time is half _____ three.

Antonyms

6. Find a list or revision word with an opposite meaning.

   (a) brother _____   (b) worse _____

   (c) adult _____   (d) slow _____

   (e) first _____   (f) before _____

   (g) mother _____   (h) thin _____

Same Sound

7. Circle the correct word.

   (a) 'We will pack (our, hour) bags and leave in one (hour, our),' said Dad.

   (b) The girl (passed, past) the ball to her friend, who was walking (past, passed) the oval.

List
sister
letter
better
butter
dinner
child
fast
last
past
glass
class
grass
ask
bath
after
afternoon
father
our

Revision
slow
drop
must
drive
here
you
roof
boy
boat
say
cold
brown
thick
sheep
spell

UNIT 10

8. Find these list words in the word search.

sister	glass
letter	class
better	grass
butter	ask
dinner	bath
child	after
afternoon	fast
father	last
our	past

s	i	s	t	e	r	f	o	r	o	g	a	l
b	o	l	a	r	u	d	g	e	h	r	i	e
d	e	r	s	s	a	l	g	t	p	a	f	t
n	w	t	r	o	k	p	l	t	u	s	n	t
n	u	s	t	e	u	t	t	u	n	s	l	e
o	b	a	d	e	f	r	i	b	n	o	t	r
o	r	p	t	u	r	e	n	n	i	d	s	e
n	r	e	t	f	a	l	h	o	y	t	l	u
r	o	a	f	o	w	l	t	c	h	i	l	d
e	w	n	a	n	a	b	a	r	q	y	e	f
t	r	o	s	s	u	l	b	c	l	a	s	s
f	r	m	t	u	t	f	a	t	h	e	r	o
a	e	l	i	n	d	y	h	i	k	h	g	o

Compound Words

9. Match the words to make a compound word.

(a) class •   • father

(b) grand •   • shave

(c) after •   • hood

(d) child •   • room

Word Challenge

10. Make as many little words as you can from the word in the box. You can rearrange the letters if you like.

> afternoon

_____

_____

_____

UNIT 11

List Words	Test 1	Test 2	Test 3	Test 4	Test 5	T
aunt						
uncle						
push						
put						
find						
mind						
kind						
about						
across						
ago						
along						
rabbit						
kitten						
puppy						
blue						
does						
even						
evening						

Look   Say   Trace   Cover   Write   Check

Difficult Words I Have Found	Test 1	Test 2	Test 3	T

Rhyming Words

1. Choose a rhyming word from your list.

   (a) shoe
   _____

   (b) song
   _____

   (c) behind
   _____

   (d) shout
   _____

   (e) boss
   _____

   (f) no
   _____

   (g) habit
   _____

My Spelling Workbook Book C

UNIT 11

2. Use list words to solve the crossword.

across

3. 2, 4 and 6 are _____ numbers
4. A young cat
8. If you look _____ the fence you will see the gate
11. Would you _____ helping to clean up?
13. _____ how many people are going to the party?
16. _____ and uncle
17. Opposite to pull

down

1. A colour
2. Early part of the night
5. An animal with large ears
6. _____ he have a new bicycle?
7. Caring
9. Can you help me _____ my lost pencil?
10. It happened a long time _____
12. _____ your rubbish in the bin
13. The bridge went _____ the river
14. Aunt and _____
15. A young dog

Alphabetical Order

3. Write these words in alphabetical order.

| blue | along | rabbit | kind |
| puppy | across | find | mind |

(a) _____   (b) _____

(c) _____   (d) _____

(e) _____   (f) _____

(g) _____   (h) _____

Spelling Challenges

- Write the words using look, say, trace, cover, write, check.
- Write the revision words in alphabetical order.
- List five more types of animals.

UNIT 11

All Mixed Up

4. Unjumble the list words.

   (a) tuan _____ (b) cunel _____

   (c) spuh _____ (d) tup _____

   (e) difn _____ (f) dimn _____

   (g) nikd _____ (h) touba _____

Antonyms

5. Find a list or revision word with an opposite meaning.

   (a) sink _____ (b) unkind _____

   (c) doesn't _____ (d) odd _____

   (e) morning _____ (f) warm _____

Synonyms

6. Find a list or revision word with a similar meaning.

   (a) bunny _____ (b) misplaced _____

   (c) discover _____ (d) helpful _____

Letters into Words

7. Write five list words using the letters in the grapes.

   _____
   _____
   _____
   _____
   _____

List
aunt
uncle
push
put
find
mind
kind
about
across
ago
along
rabbit
kitten
puppy
blue
does
even
evening

Revision
show
spot
lost
dent
they
dress
cool
toy
float
may
told
clown
moth
sheep
doll

My Spelling Workbook Book C   44   www.prim-ed.com   Prim-Ed Publishing

UNIT 11

8. Find these list words in the word search.

aunt   along
uncle   rabbit
push   kitten
put   puppy
find   blue
mind   does
kind   even
about   evening
across   ago

f	e	l	a	r	s	m	o	t	u	o	b	a
i	n	e	g	o	p	g	n	i	n	e	v	e
n	l	w	o	s	i	e	l	c	n	u	k	p
d	o	p	u	p	p	y	r	a	l	t	u	a
m	e	i	r	s	h	l	l	p	o	r	l	t
n	i	r	n	e	t	t	i	k	b	o	l	i
e	t	n	u	o	n	l	r	o	n	l	i	p
v	r	i	d	h	u	p	i	g	t	w	a	v
e	c	d	y	l	a	b	u	w	i	n	t	l
a	c	r	o	s	s	l	d	o	b	a	h	t
s	i	m	p	e	d	u	n	i	b	o	s	e
p	l	a	m	f	s	e	i	r	a	t	u	l
p	u	t	b	r	e	o	k	a	r	e	p	a

Word Meanings

9. Match each word to its meaning.

(a) aunt •   • a colour

(b) blue •   • a young dog

(c) evening •   • mother or father's sister

(d) puppy •   • the last part of the day

Read and Draw

10. (a) A puppy walking across a bridge in the evening.

    (b) A kind uncle tickling a kitten.

UNIT 12

List Words	Test 1	Test 2	Test 3	Test 4	Test 5	T
could						
would						
should						
any						
many						
baby						
body						
easy						
lady						
party						
ready						
rusty						
pretty						
happy						
funny						
carry						
hello						
nose						

Look Say Trace Cover Write Check

Difficult Words I Have Found	Test 1	Test 2	Test 3	T

Shape Sorter

1. Write a list word that fits in each shape.

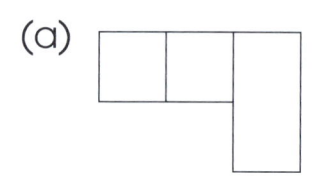

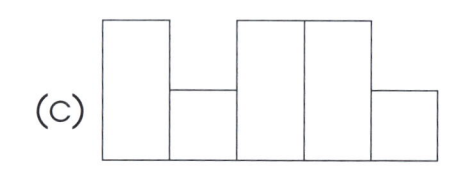

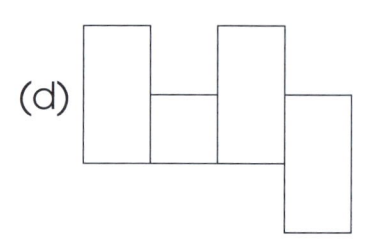

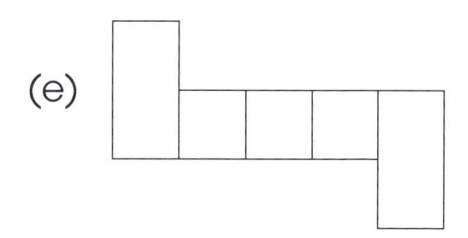

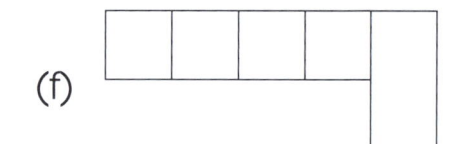

(a)
(b)
(c)
(d)
(e)
(f)

My Spelling Workbook Book C

UNIT 12

2. Use list words to solve the crossword.

across

3. A newly-born child
6. Opposite of ugly
7. Having rust on something
9. You _____ look before crossing the road
11. I _____ not see the road because it was dark
15. A greeting
16. Are there _____ lollies left?
17. _____ things make us laugh

down

1. I will help you _____ those rocks
2. Two parties, one _____
4. When will you be _____ for school?
5. Opposite of difficult
8. _____ you like to go swimming?
10. Your arm is part of your _____
12. Three ladies, one _____
13. You smell with it
14. Were there _____ people at the football match?
15. Opposite of sad

Spelling Challenges

- Write the words using look, say, trace, cover, write, check.
- Write five more words that begin with 'pr'.
- Choose five revision words and write a sentence for each.

Word Worm

3. Circle and list the words in the word worm.

_____ _____

_____ _____

_____ _____

_____

nose easy rusty could hello baby ready

UNIT 12

Compound Words

4. Match the words to make a compound word.

   (a) lady • • more _____

   (b) baby • • guard _____

   (c) any • • bird _____

   (d) body • • sit _____

Antonyms

5. Find a list or revision word with an opposite meaning.

   (a) few _____ (b) difficult _____

   (c) ugly _____ (d) sad _____

Synonyms

6. Find a list or revision word with a similar meaning.

   (a) price _____ (b) assist _____

   (c) material _____ (d) silly _____

   (e) prepared _____ (f) remain _____

Same Sound

7. Circle the correct word.

   (a) Mum asked us if we (wood, would) pick up the (wood, would) from the timber yard.

   (b) 'Who (knows, nose) the answer to the question about our (nose, knows)?' asked the teacher.

List
could
would
should
any
many
baby
body
easy
lady
party
ready
rusty
pretty
happy
funny
carry
hello
nose

Revision
bump
help
cost
bent
bell
mess
snack
joy
toast
stay
sold
rain
cloth
smash
hope

UNIT 12

8. Find these list words in the word search.

could   ready
would   rusty
should   pretty
any   funny
many   carry
baby   hello
body   lady
nose   party
happy   easy

y	r	e	v	a	l	o	u	d	l	u	o	w
m	i	r	t	o	p	r	e	t	t	y	y	o
s	o	l	l	e	h	s	l	o	m	n	n	t
b	f	s	h	o	u	l	d	m	n	a	m	o
m	r	u	s	t	y	s	h	u	r	o	n	t
b	a	l	t	p	o	n	f	e	y	d	o	b
r	e	n	l	o	a	r	e	a	s	y	s	a
d	y	o	y	u	h	r	t	l	b	v	e	r
y	d	i	l	f	a	d	t	o	n	y	m	o
b	a	h	a	m	p	l	i	y	q	r	t	y
a	e	l	d	e	p	u	s	n	o	r	a	b
n	r	t	y	b	y	o	f	e	n	a	l	a
y	a	s	t	r	l	c	b	i	v	c	a	b

Memory Master

9. Cover the list words. Write two from memory.

_____   _____

Write an interesting sentence using both words.

_____

Secret Code

10. Use the secret code to find out the list or revision word.

| 1 | 2 | 3 | 4 | 5 | 6 | 7 | 8 | 9 | 10 | 11 | 12 | 13 | 14 | 15 | 16 |
| A | B | C | D | E | H | I | K | L | O | P | R | S | T | W | Y |

(a) ___ ___ ___ ___
    2   1   2 16

(b) ___ ___ ___ ___ ___
    14 10 1 13 14

(c) ___ ___ ___ ___ ___ ___
    11 12 5 14 14 16

(d) ___ ___ ___ ___
    2 5 9 9

(e) ___ ___ ___ ___ ___
    6 1 11 11 16

(f) ___ ___ ___ ___ ___
    12 5 1 4 16

UNIT 13

List Words	Test 1	Test 2	Test 3	Test 4	Test 5	T
where						
why						
what						
who						
goes						
going						
gone						
air						
pair						
hair						
chair						
fair						
fairy						
stairs						
kneel						
know						
knew						
knife						

Look Say Trace Cover Write Check

Difficult Words I Have Found	Test 1	Test 2	Test 3	T

Same Sound

1. Circle the correct word to match the picture.

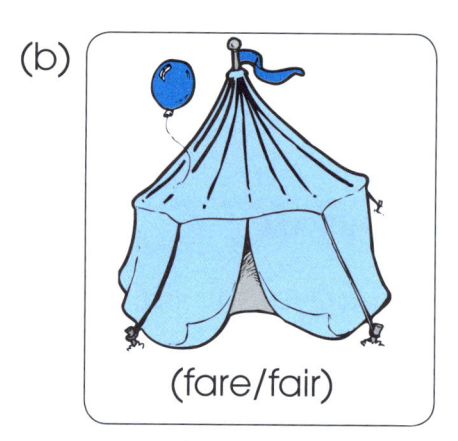

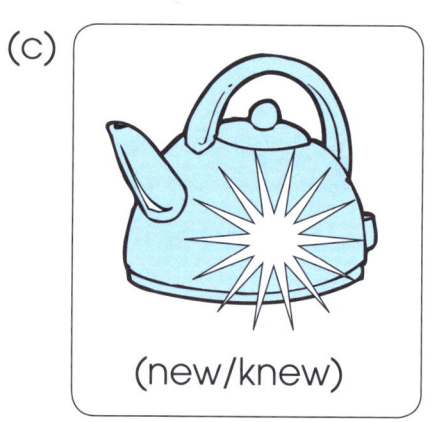

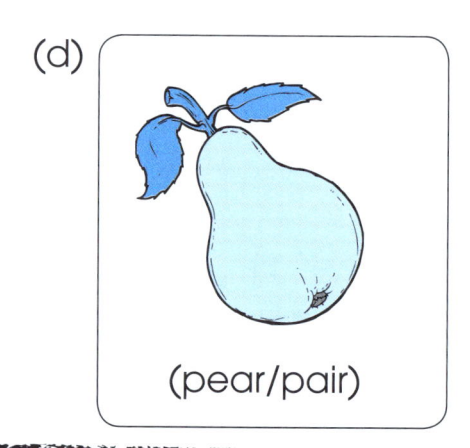

(a) (hair/hare)

(b) (fare/fair)

(c) (new/knew)

(d) (pear/pair)

My Spelling Workbook Book C — www.prim-ed.com — Prim-Ed Publishing

UNIT 13

2. Use list words to solve the crossword.

across

1. _____ is the matter with you?
2. To place your weight on your knees
3. I am not _____ home yet
5. Something you sit on
8. _____ are all the new pencils?
9. You can walk up them
10. A magical creature
11. Do you _____ the answer to that question?
12. We breathe it
13. All the children have _____ home

down

1. Did you see _____ came first?
2. A _____ and fork
4. Who _____ to music lessons after school?
6. Found on your head
7. Two of something
8. A word that asks a question
10. A blonde has _____ hair
11. He _____ the answer to the question

Alphabetical Order

3. Put these list words into alphabetical order.

| fair | know | who | chair |
| kneel | stairs | pair | air |

(a) _____   (b) _____
(c) _____   (d) _____
(e) _____   (f) _____
(g) _____   (h) _____

Spelling Challenges

- Write the words using look, say, trace, cover, write, check.
- Write the revision list in alphabetical order.
- Write a new word that sounds the same as the words below:
  tied, bear, here, flour, ball.

UNIT 13

Rhyming Words

4. Write the list words that rhyme with 'air'.

   (a) _____ (b) _____

   (c) _____ (d) _____

   (e) _____

All Mixed Up

5. (a) awth _____ (b) traiss _____

   (c) soeg _____ (d) yhw _____

   (e) reehw _____ (f) kelen _____

   (g) fekin _____ (h) nigog _____

Antonyms

6. Find a list or revision word with an opposite meaning.

   (a) coming _____ (b) front _____

   (c) right _____ (d) unfair _____

   (e) start _____ (f) buy _____

Same Sound

7. Circle the correct word.

   (a) The children decided to (where, wear) their swimming costume to (where, wear) they were going.

   (b) The (pear, pare, pair) of farmers caught the (hair, hare) in the forest.

   (c) The (fare, fair)-haired child paid his (fair, fare) as the driver asked, 'Are you (new, knew) here?'.

List
where
why
what
who
goes
going
gone
air
pair
hair
chair
fair
fairy
stairs
kneel
know
knew
knife

Revision
spend
left
stop
tent
sell
loss
back
than
load
way
gold
train
with
crush
note

UNIT 13

8. Find these list words in the word search.

where	chair
why	fair
what	fairy
who	stairs
goes	kneel
going	know
gone	knew
air	knife
pair	hair

s	p	e	n	o	g	o	r	m	o	f	l	t
t	h	a	i	b	i	o	u	t	m	l	g	s
a	w	r	s	t	e	n	g	e	f	i	n	k
i	m	i	l	s	r	a	s	p	t	k	i	t
r	f	a	w	h	e	k	g	a	p	l	o	n
s	w	h	e	k	h	n	a	i	r	n	g	t
w	h	c	n	a	w	e	p	r	l	n	w	o
k	o	h	k	l	n	e	b	r	f	a	i	r
o	n	a	i	e	w	l	n	e	k	w	o	b
d	h	o	l	y	h	w	h	a	g	a	s	t
s	t	a	w	r	a	i	t	l	r	o	b	m
p	s	t	i	n	f	a	i	r	y	l	e	d
w	h	a	t	r	u	l	i	n	p	s	t	s

Missing Words

9. Complete, using one of these list words.

| Where | knew | pair | goes |

(a) She _____ to tennis on Saturdays.

(b) He _____ that the puppy was lost.

(c) _____ is your pencil case?

(d) May I have a _____ of gloves?

Building Words

10. Join 'kn' with an ending to make a word.

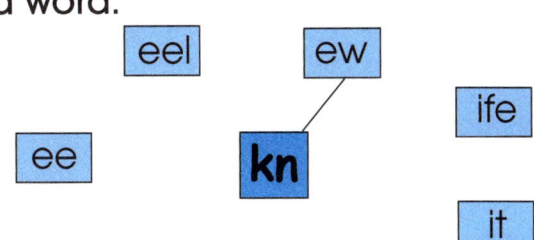

eel   ew
ee   kn   ife
ot   ow   it

knew
_____
_____
_____
_____
_____
_____

UNIT 14

List Words	Test 1	Test 2	Test 3	Test 4	Test 5	T
talk						
walk						
two						
once						
paw						
draw						
school						
garden						
getting						
morning						
new						
these						
their						
stalk						
wash						
watch						
buy						
pull						

Look Say Trace Cover Write Check

Difficult Words I Have Found	Test 1	Test 2	Test 3	T

Word Hunt

1. (a) Which list words end in 'ing'?

   _____

   _____

   (b) Which list words have double letters?

   _____

   _____

   _____

   (c) Which revision word means the same as 'healthy'?

   _____

   (d) Which list words rhyme with 'saw'?

   _____

   _____

UNIT 14

2. Use list words to solve the crossword.

across

3. A place of learning
4. Who is _____ the lunches?
7. Opposite to old
9. Can you _____ a picture of a farm?
10. Are _____ your new clothes?
11. Half of four
16. We are going to the shops to _____ a new radio
17. Everyone had to give a _____ on his or her favourite hobby

down

1. Comes before afternoon
2. _____ upon a time
4. A place for growing plants
5. A clock worn on the wrist
6. Is that _____ new car?
8. You should always _____ your hands before a meal
12. When the car broke down we had to _____ home
13. The lions had to _____ their prey
14. Opposite to push
15. The dog licked her _____

Spelling Sums

3. (a) morn + ing = _____
   (b) gar + den = _____
   (c) w + atch = _____
   (d) dr + aw = _____
   (e) get + ting = _____
   (f) sch + ool = _____
   (g) st + alk = _____
   (h) th + ere = _____

Spelling Challenges

- Write the words using look, say, trace, cover, write, check.
- Write five more words that begin with 'th'.
- Choose five list words and write a sentence for each.

UNIT 14

Word Meanings

4. Match each word to its meaning.

   (a) two •   • part of a flower

   (b) watch •   • a dog's foot

   (c) stalk •   • tells the time

   (d) paw •   • one less than three

Antonyms

5. Find a list or revision word with an opposite meaning.

   (a) evening _____ (b) sell _____

   (c) well _____ (d) push _____

Synonyms

6. Find a list or revision word with the same meaning.

   (a) chat _____ (b) stroll _____

   (c) fix _____ (d) throw _____

   (e) sweep _____ (f) clock _____

Changing Words

7. Change one letter in each word to make a list word.

   (a) law ➔ _____

   (b) sew ➔ _____

   (c) wall ➔ _____

   (d) too ➔ _____

   (e) but ➔ _____

   (f) stall ➔ _____

List

talk
walk
two
once
paw
draw
school
garden
getting
morning
new
these
their
stalk
wash
watch
buy
pull

Revision

mend
sick
stand
sent
well
toss
tone
that
road
play
hold
tail
cake
brush
home

My Spelling Workbook Book C · 56 · www.prim-ed.com · Prim-Ed Publishing

UNIT 14

8. **Find these list words in the word search.**

talk   morning
walk   new
these two
their once
stalk paw
wash   draw
watch school
buy   garden
pull   getting

e	t	h	r	w	e	n	b	t	w	y	e	g
v	w	h	c	h	c	t	a	w	e	i	n	a
c	o	n	s	e	h	e	w	a	r	d	o	r
p	i	c	w	s	c	h	o	o	l	r	g	d
t	w	t	h	e	s	e	b	a	t	e	r	e
o	n	g	b	i	t	r	i	e	t	u	m	n
g	n	i	u	o	n	e	f	t	s	w	b	k
n	o	c	y	w	c	h	i	h	r	a	i	l
i	s	e	e	r	o	n	t	e	r	p	o	a
n	i	k	o	w	g	n	a	i	p	t	l	t
r	e	l	g	i	a	o	d	r	o	n	i	s
o	n	a	t	a	w	s	o	e	k	l	a	w
m	u	t	p	u	l	l	h	h	e	i	s	e

Antonyms

9. **Count the syllables.**

   (a) new _1_   (b) two _____

   (c) school _____ (d) garden _____

   (e) morning _____ (f) getting _____

What am I?

10. (a) I can't talk but I am often noisy.

    I have many books.

    You come to me to learn.

    I am a _____

    (b) I am many colours but mostly green.

    Birds and insects visit me.

    You like to play in me.

    I am a _____

UNIT 15

List Words	Test 1	Test 2	Test 3	Test 4	Test 5	T
over						
next						
more						
present						
football						
grandfather						
grandmother						
inside						
outside						
myself						
herself						
himself						
somebody						
someone						
something						
sometimes						
holiday						
bedroom						

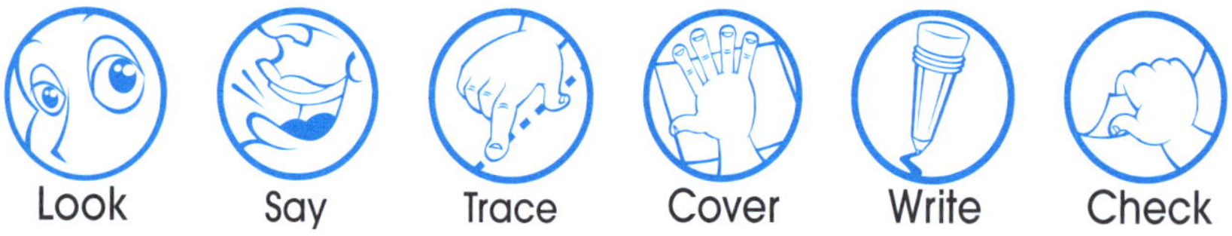

Look Say Trace Cover Write Check

Difficult Words I Have Found	Test 1	Test 2	Test 3	T

Missing Letters

1. (a) m__o__ __r__e

   more

   (b) i__s__ __e

   (c) h__ms__ __f

   (d) __o__ __d__y

   (e) __oot__a__

   (f) __ __x__

   (g) m__se__ __

   (h) __o__ __on__

My Spelling Workbook Book C

UNIT 15

2. Use list words to solve the crossword.

across

1. The room in which you sleep
4. Opposite to under
6. A gift
8. _____ and grandfather
12. A sport that uses a ball
13. _____ at school lost their new school bag
15. Opposite of herself
16. Opposite of outside
17. Opposite of himself

down

2. Opposite of less
3. It's my birthday _____ week
5. _____ and grandmother
7. The boy threw _____ at the bird
9. Opposite of inside
10. _____ it is too wet to play
11. A break from work or school
13. Similar to 'someone'
14. I had to walk home by _____

Spelling Challenges

- Write the words using look, say, trace, cover, write, check.
- Write five more compound words that end in _____ 'ball'.
- Write the revision list in alphabetical order.

Prim-Ed Publishing   www.prim-ed.com   59   My Spelling Workbook Book C

UNIT 15

Small Words

3. Find small words in these list words.

   (a) present _____

   (b) holiday _____

   (c) bedroom _____

   (d) someone _____

   (e) inside _____

All Mixed Up

4. (a) oderbom _____ (b) rome _____

   (c) revo _____ (d) lesfimh _____

Antonyms

5. Find a list or revision word with an opposite meaning.

   (a) under _____ (b) less _____

   (c) absent _____ (d) outside _____

Synonyms

6. Find a list or revision word with the same meaning.

   (a) gift _____ (b) me _____

   (c) vacation _____ (d) close _____

Memory Master

7. Cover the list words. Write two from memory.

   _____   _____

   Write an interesting sentence using both words.

   _____

   _____

List
over
next
more
present
football
grandfather
grandmother
inside
outside
myself
herself
himself
somebody
someone
something
sometimes
holiday
bedroom

Revision
lend
sock
shut
lent
fell
cross
cone
them
hay
which
bait
fern
fill
just
loaf

UNIT 15

8. Find these list words in the word search.

over   herself
next   himself
more   somebody
present   someone
football   something
holiday   inside
bedroom   outside
myself
grandfather
sometimes
grandmother

g	s	t	r	s	e	m	i	t	e	m	o	s
r	e	o	l	l	a	b	t	o	o	f	u	d
a	h	i	m	s	e	l	f	o	m	i	t	r
n	a	t	n	e	s	e	r	p	d	y	s	e
d	m	f	o	t	b	e	m	t	h	o	i	h
m	r	i	l	m	o	o	r	d	e	b	d	t
o	e	t	h	e	r	g	d	n	r	e	e	a
t	v	o	l	e	s	s	a	y	s	n	b	f
h	o	l	i	d	a	y	b	e	e	o	n	d
e	d	n	e	x	t	o	m	e	l	e	g	n
r	e	n	i	n	s	i	d	e	f	m	r	a
g	n	d	t	h	n	g	b	o	r	o	e	r
s	o	m	e	t	h	i	n	g	i	s	e	g

Compound Words

9. Match the words to make a compound word.

(a) foot • • noon
(b) lady • • self
(c) grand • • bird
(d) no • • ball
(e) bed • • side
(f) out • • thing
(g) after • • room
(h) my • • father

Read and Draw

10. (a) A grandfather kicking a football in his bedroom.

(b) A clown opening a present on holiday.

UNIT 16

List Words	Test 1	Test 2	Test 3	Test 4	Test 5	T
door						
poor						
floor						
eye						
nearly						
friend						
says						
paper						
river						
summer						
winter						
number						
queen						
quick						
break						
great						
word						
work						

Look Say Trace Cover Write Check

Difficult Words I Have Found	Test 1	Test 2	Test 3	T

Rhyming Words

1. Choose a rhyming word from your list.

   (a) been _____

   (b) ate _____

   (c) spend _____

   (d) bye _____

   (e) more _____

   (f) stick _____

   (g) steak _____

   (h) bird _____

My Spelling Workbook Book C   62   www.prim-ed.com   Prim-Ed Publishing

UNIT 16

2. Use list words to solve the crossword.

across

5. Almost
6. A large stream
9. You open this before you walk through it
10. King and _____
11. Opposite of enemy
15. If you drop a glass it might _____
16. Good

down

1. Opposite of winter
2. Used to see with
3. Don't slip on the wet _____
4. The cold season
7. Opposite of rich
8. Which _____ did you misspell?
10. Opposite of slow
12. What _____ comes between seven and nine?
13. You have to _____ to earn a living
14. You write on it

Spelling Challenges

- Write the words using look, say, trace, cover, write, check.
- Write five more words that begin with 'qu'.
- Choose five list words and write a sentence for each.

Shape Sorter

3. Write a list word that fits in each shape.

(a)

(b)

(c)

(d)

(e)

UNIT 16

Missing Words

List: door, poor, floor, eye, nearly, friend, says, paper, river, summer, winter, number, queen, quick, break, great, word, work

4. Complete using one of these list words.

   word   number   river   summer   nearly

   (a) We go to the beach in the _____ holidays.

   (b) What _____ comes before six?

   (c) She _____ fell off her bike.

   (d) What _____ rhymes with seat?

   (e) The fish swam in the _____.

Antonyms

5. Find a list or revision word with an opposite meaning.

   (a) rich _____   (b) foe _____

   (c) repair _____   (d) worst _____

Synonyms

6. Find a list or revision word with a similar meaning.

   (a) almost _____   (b) destroy _____

   (c) fast _____   (d) happy _____

Same Sound

7. Circle the correct word.

   (a) The (poor, paw) boy's dog had a sore (paw, poor).

   (b) The (floor, flaw) in the wood caused the (floor, flaw) to sag.

   (c) The (great, grate) in the open fire was a (great, grate) big piece of iron.

Revision: glad, best, shed, hill, tell, three, rope, call, soak, lay, whip, wait, her, still, fall

UNIT 16

8. Find these list words in the word search.

door	winter
poor	number
floor	queen
eye	quick
nearly	break
friend	great
says	word
paper	work
river	summer

r	e	r	o	c	r	k	l	r	e	d	n	u
e	m	o	t	h	i	b	e	r	k	o	d	w
t	l	o	a	y	v	i	r	e	b	m	u	n
n	i	d	e	b	e	d	r	o	w	u	q	t
i	o	o	r	k	r	e	y	i	b	r	u	h
w	e	s	g	h	m	e	a	t	f	e	i	s
r	a	t	u	l	p	r	a	d	l	s	c	e
r	o	o	p	m	n	e	l	k	o	a	k	d
e	w	o	r	k	m	e	y	e	o	y	p	n
n	e	a	m	c	u	e	a	h	r	s	l	e
e	p	a	p	e	r	o	r	r	t	s	l	i
f	d	r	i	e	t	w	n	i	l	t	e	r
q	u	e	e	n	b	e	r	n	u	y	r	f

Word Hunt

9. (a) Which list words end with 'er'?

   _____ _____ _____

   _____ _____

   (b) Which revision words end in 'll'?

   _____ _____ _____

   _____ _____

   (c) Which list words rhyme with 'more'?

   _____ _____ _____

   (d) Which list words begin with 'qu'?

   _____ _____

What am I?

10. I have many names.

    I play with you.

    I listen.

    I am a

    _____

UNIT 17

List Words	Test 1	Test 2	Test 3	Test 4	Test 5	T
shoe						
seven						
also						
hook						
dull						
upon						
rung						
hung						
wind						
bear						
peek						
cheek						
asleep						
most						
both						
host						
forever						
clever						

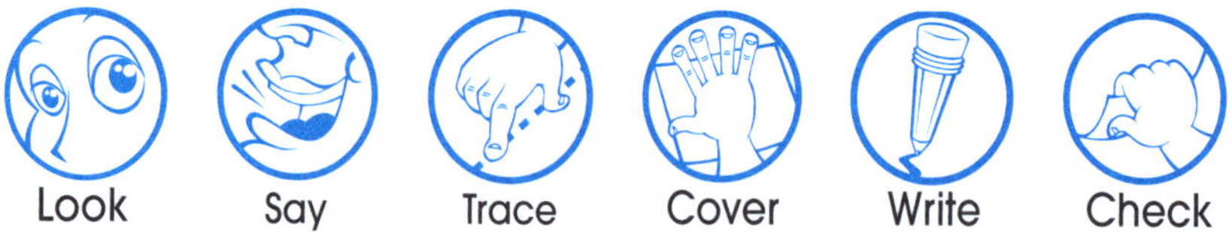

Look Say Trace Cover Write Check

Difficult Words I Have Found	Test 1	Test 2	Test 3	T

Letters into Words

1. Write five list words using the letters in the cloud.

   (cloud contains: h, t, o, b, m, r, g, u, n, s)

   _____
   _____
   _____
   _____
   _____

Word Hunt

2. (a) Which list word rhymes with book?
   _____

   (b) Which list word means the opposite of awake?
   _____

My Spelling Workbook Book C

3. Use list words to solve the crossword.

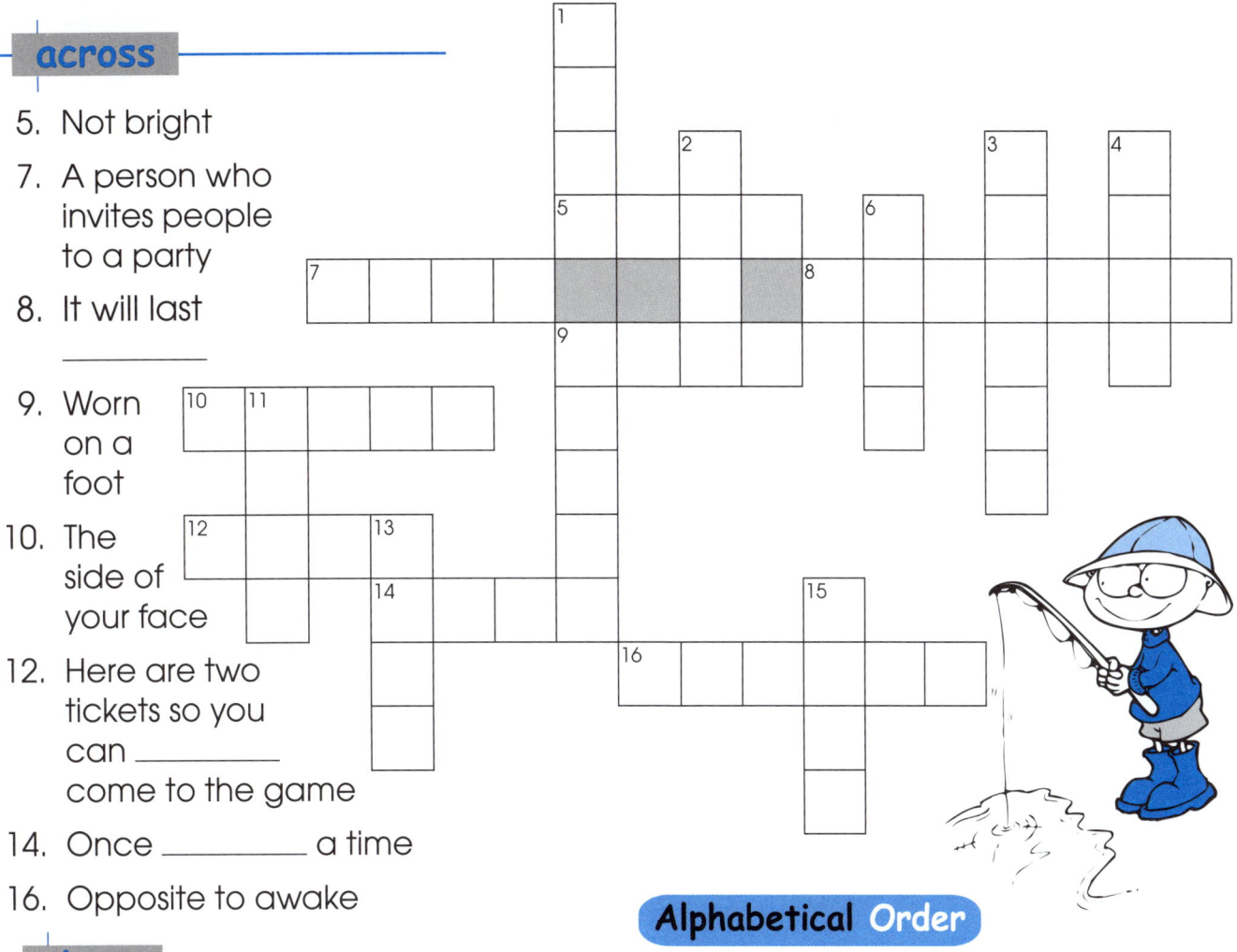

across

5. Not bright
7. A person who invites people to a party
8. It will last _____
9. Worn on a foot
10. The side of your face
12. Here are two tickets so you can _____ come to the game
14. Once _____ a time
16. Opposite to awake

down

1. Breeze
2. As well
3. Smart
4. To take a quick look
6. Nearly all
9. Half of 14
11. Used in fishing
13. The boy _____ up his wet raincoat before coming inside
15. A large furry animal

Alphabetical Order

4. Put these words into alphabetical order.

| bear | dull | shoe | seven |
| clever | also | host | most |

_____ _____

_____ _____

_____ _____

_____ _____

Spelling Challenges

- Write the words using look, say, trace, cover, write, check.
- Write five more words with the 'ee' sound.
- Choose five revision words and write a sentence for each.

UNIT 17

All Mixed Up

5. Unjumble the list words.

   (a) neves _____ (b) soeh _____

   (c) okoh _____ (d) sola _____

   (e) ludl _____ (f) ponu _____

   (g) diwn _____ (h) gunh _____

Word Meanings

6. Match the word to its correct meaning.

   (a) rung •   • used to hang things

   (b) host •   • to turn or twist something

   (c) hook •   • part of a ladder

   (d) wind •   • a person who entertains

Antonyms

7. Find a list or revision word with an opposite meaning.

   (a) bright _____ (b) least _____

   (c) awake _____ (d) foolish _____

Same Sound

8. Circle the correct word.

   (a) 'The apple tree will (bear, bare) fruit this year,' said Dad.

   (b) '(They're, Their, There) you are,' said the little girl as she found her lost cat.

List
shoe
seven
also
hook
dull
upon
rung
hung
wind
bear
peek
cheek
asleep
most
both
host
forever
clever

Revision
hall
tall
ink
sink
drink
pay
girl
first
fork
born
May
forgot
owl
frown
sail

UNIT 17

9. Find these list words in the word search.

shoe	peek
seven	cheek
also	asleep
hook	most
dull	both
upon	host
rung	forever
hung	clever
wind	bear

k	e	e	h	c	r	i	c	k	d	n	i	w
o	o	c	l	e	v	e	r	e	o	n	u	m
d	w	n	g	n	u	r	v	e	l	o	p	o
h	u	n	g	e	e	p	r	p	o	p	a	s
e	b	e	r	h	o	s	t	t	r	u	m	t
t	h	o	e	a	l	s	o	t	b	v	e	r
h	a	w	t	r	r	m	o	e	s	t	m	o
d	u	l	l	h	l	o	a	t	h	b	r	b
o	p	k	u	o	e	r	t	n	e	v	e	s
e	l	d	h	o	w	o	t	e	d	e	r	t
o	l	l	u	k	o	v	e	s	t	u	n	h
h	e	s	f	o	r	e	v	e	r	r	l	d
s	w	t	a	s	l	e	e	p	r	o	e	l

Missing Words

10. Complete, using one of these list words.

| clever | bear | cheek | seven | upon |

(a) A part of your face is your _____.

(b) The word smart is a synonym of _____.

(c) A large, furry animal is a _____.

(d) The number before eight is _____.

(e) Stories often start with 'Once _____ a time'.

Word Worm

11. Circle and list the words in the word worm.

mostalsocleverwindrungcheekasleephook

_____
_____
_____

UNIT 18

List Words	Test 1	Test 2	Test 3	Test 4	Test 5	T
fried						
cried						
cries						
visit						
fence						
thorn						
too						
care						
port						
story						
doctor						
only						
open						
head						
bread						
large						
climb						
half						

Look Say Trace Cover Write Check

Difficult Words I Have Found	Test 1	Test 2	Test 3	T

Small Words

1. Find small words in these list words.

(a) thorn

_____

(b) care

_____

(c) only

_____

(d) open

_____

(e) head

_____

(f) climb

_____

(g) bread

_____

My Spelling Workbook Book C

UNIT 18

2. Use list words to solve the crossword.

across

2. Did you see that monkey _____ the tree?
4. One of two equal parts
6. Shouts
9. A place for ships
10. The children were so upset that they _____
14. A sharp barb on a plant
15. A tale
16. Very big

down

1. Helps sick people
3. Keeps things in or out
4. Part of your body
5. I like _____ eggs
6. To show love for
7. Opposite of shut
8. Did you _____ your friends yesterday?
11. _____ three people may go
12. Used to make a sandwich
13. It was _____ cold to go swimming

Spelling Challenges

- Write the words using look, say, trace, cover, write, check.
- Write four more 'or' words.
- Write the revision list in alphabetical order.

Missing Letters

3. (a) t___ ___rn

(b) ___al___

(c) c ___ ___es

(d) ___t___r___

(e) v___s___t

UNIT 18

Mixed up Sentences

4. Unjumble the sentences.

   (a) fence! the Don't climb

   _____

   (b) doctor. your Ask

   _____

   (c) too Half much. is

   _____

Antonyms

5. Find a list or revision word with an opposite meaning.

   (a) laughed _____   (b) close _____

   (c) small _____   (d) up _____

Synonyms

6. Find a list or revision word with a similar meaning.

   (a) harbour _____   (b) tale _____

   (c) big _____   (d) small _____

Same Sound

7. Circle the correct word.

   (a) (Too, Two, To) players went (to, two, too) pick up the ball but it was (too, to, two) late.

   (b) The well (bred, bread) horse enjoyed eating (bread, bred) with its feed.

List
fried
cried
cries
visit
fence
thorn
too
care
port
story
doctor
only
open
head
bread
large
climb
half

Revision
wall
goat
think
pink
wink
third
bird
shirt
dirt
torn
short
fold
down
nail
snail

My Spelling Workbook Book C   72   www.prim-ed.com   Prim-Ed Publishing

UNIT 18

8. Find these list words in the word search.

fried	doctor
cried	only
cries	open
visit	head
fence	bread
thorn	large
too	climb
care	half
port	story

c	r	c	h	i	e	t	o	y	r	o	t	s
r	e	l	d	o	c	t	o	r	n	e	o	p
i	v	i	t	s	n	l	n	r	o	h	t	r
e	l	m	o	n	e	b	r	e	a	g	r	e
s	t	b	n	o	f	d	o	g	e	r	a	l
f	h	o	l	f	e	a	k	c	r	i	e	d
t	o	o	y	m	e	e	h	w	o	b	r	e
e	n	c	e	f	r	h	t	a	g	p	l	y
l	a	r	g	e	o	p	r	v	l	o	e	m
c	e	h	t	o	m	w	o	h	i	f	e	n
a	d	o	m	b	y	r	p	l	e	s	a	m
r	f	r	i	e	d	o	m	g	e	b	i	l
e	s	i	r	e	a	l	d	a	e	r	b	t

Memory Master

9. Cover the list words. Write two from memory.

_____   _____

Write an interesting sentence using both words.

_____

Secret Code

10. Use the secret code to find out the list or revision word.

1	2	3	4	5	6	7
A	C	D	E	F	G	H
8	9	10	11	12	13	14
I	L	N	O	R	S	T

(a) ___ ___ ___ ___ ___
     5   4 10   2   4

(b) ___ ___ ___ ___
     7   1   9   5

(c) ___ ___ ___
    14 11 11

(d) ___ ___ ___ ___ ___ ___
     3 11   2 14 11 12

(e) ___ ___ ___ ___ ___
     2 12   8   4   3

(f) ___ ___ ___ ___ ___
     9   1 12   6   4

Interesting Words from my Writing

Date	Word	Date	Word	Date	Word
Date	Word	Date	Word	Date	Word

Interesting Words from my Writing

Date	Word	Date	Word	Date	Word

My Dictionary Words: Aa to Ii

Aa	Bb	Cc
Dd	Ee	Ff
Gg	Hh	Ii

My Dictionary Words: Jj to Rr

Jj

Kk

Ll

Mm

Nn

Oo

Pp

Qq

Rr

My Dictionary Words: Ss to Zz

Ss

Tt

Uu

Vv

Ww

Xx

Yy

Zz